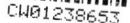

salmonpoetry

Diverse Voices from Ireland and the World

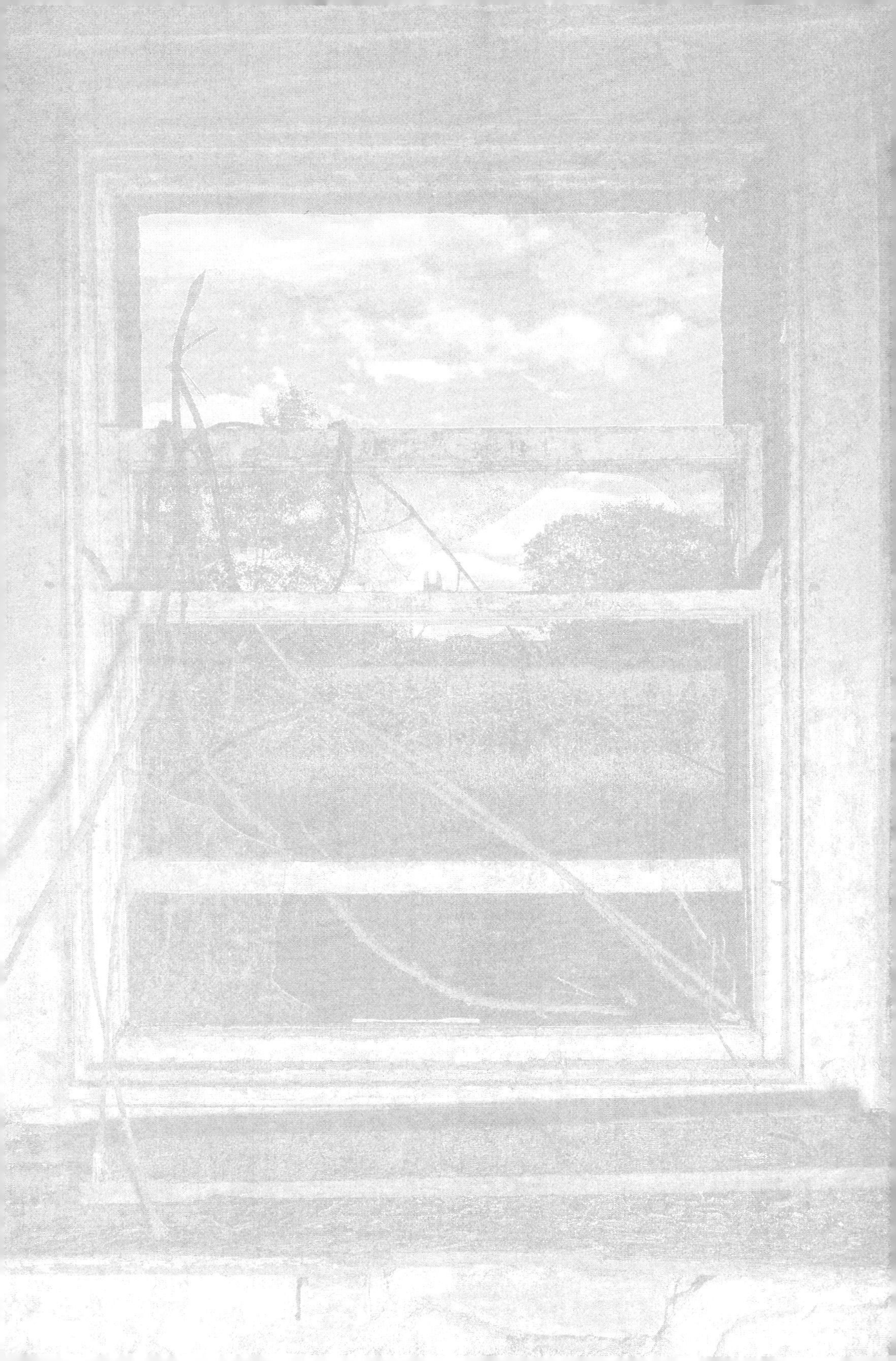

Moving On

Poems by
PHIL LYNCH

salmonpoetry

Published in 2024 by
Salmon Poetry
Cliffs of Moher, County Clare, Ireland
Website: www.salmonpoetry.com
Email: info@salmonpoetry.com

Copyright © Philip Lynch, 2024

ISBN 978-1-915022-62-2

All rights reserved. No part of this publication may be reproduced or transmitted in any form or by any means, electronic or mechanical, including photography, recording, or any information storage or retrieval system, without permission in writing from the publisher. The book is sold subject to the condition that it shall not, by way of trade or otherwise, be lent, resold or otherwise circulated without the publisher's prior consent in any form of binding or cover other than that in which it is published and without a similar condition, including this condition, being imposed on the subsequent purchaser.

Cover & Title Page Image: *Donal Norton*
Cover Design & Typesetting: Siobhán Hutson
Author Photo: Carl Roche Portraits

Printed in Ireland by Sprint Print

Salmon Poetry gratefully acknowledges the support of
The Arts Council / An Chomhairle Ealaíon

*For Mary, Eimear, Caroline,
Hazel, Esme and Liza (not forgetting Kevin)
my brothers Tom, Sean and Jim*

*and to honour the memory of my parents
Michael (Bap) Lynch (1914-1995)
Mary B. Lynch (nee Norton) (1916-1992)*

Contents

	Page
Angles	11
Stepping Stones	12
Sudden Fall	13
Closed	14
Future History	16
Re-Entry	17
drifters	22
Absence	23
Travels Back and Forth	24
Dancers	30
Reading the Sundays	31
A Game of Two Halves	33
August	34
Flashback	35
Journey	36
Roll Call	37
Harvesting	38
summer song	40
Learning to Swim	41
Lightning Strike	42
moments	43
Awaiting News	44
Nocturne	46
From Notes made at Camden Lock	47
made to last	50
Moving On	51
Déjà vu	52
Whispers	54
Lines	55
Undelivered	56
Longshots	57

A Bit of Bad Language	58
The Reading and the Recital	59
In-Betweenness	61
Wintering	63
Words on the Street	64
Outsiders	65
Direct Knowledge	66
ask	67
Lullaby to a Lost Future	68
The Morning After	69
Transformed	70
In a Spin	71
Surge	72
Storm Warning	73
Christmas Craic	74
Let the New Light In	75
Victory Flight	76
This is a day the dead would like	77
All You Can Do	78
Core Value	79
Running	80
overheard by trees	81
Night Shift	82
ups & downs	83
Footage	84
In the Middle of the Woods	85
kindling	86
Notes	89
Acknowledgements	90
About the Author	92

Angles

Light casts
   many
         different
               shadows,
how we see them
depends on where we stand.

Stepping Stones

We hop on stepping stones
to cross the river on the way
home from school and where the water
narrows its furrow, we learn, through
bets, dares and bravado, to jump
from bank to bank.

We run free-spirited as the rain
through wild-flowered fields,
climbing gates, jumping stiles,
we are high jumpers and pole-vaulters,
riders of bucking broncos,
playing cowboys and Indians, cops
and robbers, spies and spy-catchers,
goodies and baddies all in one day.

The only barrier to our stride
is when it comes to sleep.
Even then our minds continue
to chase adventure of all kinds –

snipers on the loose
near the house, we dive to hide
behind a giant clamp of turf,
something moves inside the shed,
a head pops out and shouts
you're dead –

when light creeps back
to tap the glass, we crank up
our boisterous engines and mingle
with the whirr and rattle of machines
at work, the beat of barking dogs
and all the other moving parts of life
being lightly lived, oblivious
of the burden weighing
on the ones who make it hum.

Sudden Fall

The leaves fell on Saturday,
succumbing to the firm force
of a sudden September storm.

Autumn had come unannounced,
awkward, an uninvited guest
at an intimate dinner party.

The ground a confusion of greens,
many in their prime, smooth to the touch,
clinging to the illusion of foreverness.

Nature took care to sprinkle them
with a camouflage of half-turned reds and yellows
to lighten the shame, share in the shock.

The trees stood bereft in the after-calm,
stoic in the stillness of silent thought,
uncertain what to expect next, a feast or a fall.

Closed

No train or public bus came near,
though at times it seemed all roads
converged as if it were a busy station,
this isolated heart of a remote place.

Nothing left but broken shelves
once filled with sweets and bread
and cigarettes, unfiltered,
unlike the seditious conversations
held in corners out of reach
in breach of normal protocols.
Strangers often tramped the roads,
stopping for a mug of milk and a look
at that day's paper, in search perhaps
of some secret code.

At parties filled with songs
and late-night storytelling,
neighbours traded gossip
in the kindliest of unkind ways.
Sour dregs of bottled stout drained
when all was quiet, like now,
when new ghosts joined their kindred ranks
to trip up future passers-by
or tap them on the shoulder
like an acorn dropping from a tree.

Only those who had seen its glory
could understand the loss behind
each strangled branch of sweet-smelling
blackberry bush, abandoned flower beds
and buried pathways that led
to prairies, plains and battlefields,
steps that turned into stages,
hollow ditches a cover for first smokes,
supplies hidden among stones,
where thoughts of love once bloomed.

All smothered in the undergrowth
save for a few rescued relics
and skeleton accounts of events known,
the unknown forever lost.

Future History

What will we become
by which our children's children and beyond
will know us when we are gone?

Things that have not been made or named,
new ways to live and cure and kill,
will become the new old in our children's time.

They will talk fondly of us and wonder
what we would make of the new new
as they reflect on how so much has changed.

Their children will recount fun times
they had with us and tell nostalgic tales
of escapades with extra nuggets of embellishment.

They will regret we never made a trip
to space, though always looking at the stars,
we never got to see our planet from afar.

The children of our children's children
will rarely speak our names and only know
a thing or two to which they can relate –

the place we lived, the year we died – the rest
they may access for family research
from data archive stations orbiting the earth.

They may reflect about how sad it was
we thought our earthly world held all
the life there was – if only we had known.

From then on, we will seldom, if ever,
be mentioned, except perhaps as the forebears
of some famous or infamous descendant.

Re-Entry

I

My mother kept a diary,
it was mostly of the weather
with a fragrance of the flowers
she tended in her garden.

Her diaries lay in darkness
a quarter of a century
at the bottom of her wardrobe
where none had gone to enter.

Snapshots of the doings of the day,
the comings and the goings
of family and neighbours
their chores and various ailments.

Religious duties duly done,
confessions, masses, missions,
marriages, funerals, and other
ceremonial occasions listed.

Meetings, which were many,
reveal a record of involvement,
teaching, ICA, choir-leading,
church business, charity work.

II
Some days recorded in a single word,
ironed, churned, thresher, showers,
other days in two, *cleaned presses,*
washed hair, washed clothes, made jam.

Another day, *did nothing much.*
There is mention too of letters
received, written and despatched.
Most of her entries are *as Gaeilge.*

The global interrupts the local,
dúnmharaíodh S. F. O Cinnéide i Dallas
is referenced in passing on the date
that decades later would mark her own farewell.

The first moon landing is recorded
on a Monday that had the look of rain.
My own lift-off to another country
is entered on a cold day in August;

that I left for Belgium at 4.15, is noted
on the day after Hurricane Charley.
On her visits with my father, trips to Ypres,
Keukenhof, Clervaux and La Roche stand out.

as Gaeilge: in the Irish (Gaelic) language

dúnmharaíodh S. F. O Cinnéide i Dallas: JFK (John FitzGerald Kennedy) was murdered in Dallas

III
I search the pages for entries
of other memories brought to mind.
The gaps I find make dates uncertain,
the imprint of events as vivid as ever.

The seaside excitement of Laytown,
the two of us in a guest house,
when she brought me into Butlin's
through a fence at the back of the woods

or the time we were in Belfast
when she went to see a prisoner
and persisted in speaking Irish
until the guards refused us entry.

The Sunday we were alone at home
while the rest of them were at late mass,
as we went about our ritual tasks –
sweeping, dusting, polishing, shining –

I made her promise not to get mad
at me or shout like a teacher in class
before I asked her if I could keep
my new Sunday clothes on all day;

one of our more intimate moments.
I remember how she looked at me
half shocked, half stifling laughter
and after a forever pause, gave in.

Her telling the story to neighbours
made her laugh and made me happy
as she put me in the hero role,
a bond unspoken, set to last.

Another day, together in church,
she cajoled me to pick up a purse
dropped by a neighbour two rows up,
bribe as she might, I was too shy to budge.

And the way she used to scare me
with throwaway talk of dying –
at mention of future events she'd say,
I don't know if I'll live that long.

One day she took a weakness
that sent me running for my father –
we raced back to the house,
my heart a cartwheel of fear.

I was too scared to follow him
through the dark and gaping door.
Her turn passed, but not the thought
that her dying-talk was real.

IV

Half a lifetime later, at a lecture in Leuven
on Ireland's cultural history,
word came through of her sudden attack.
This time it was far too far to run.

We had spoken on the phone
the night before, she was looking
forward to my father's coming home
from hospital after surgery.

Flights scrambled while kids at school.
One of the longest days. Seven months
since she had noted our last parting,
just after teatime on a dry April evening.

There was no need to record
how much it rained at her funeral,
it is ingrained in the memory of that day,
a perfect camouflage for our tears.

She hovers over the pages now
as clear as her trademark hand
that wrapped up each day's events
with a neat line before she slept.

*pianta im bhrollach go minic
agus go holc* she wrote
before her final entry full of hope
for the homecoming to come.

pianta im bhrollach go minic agus go holc = frequent
and bad pains in my chest

drifters

we are drifters shifting
    in shadows of doubt lost
        in a landscape of half-withered thought

we talk to everyone and no one
    we argue with ourselves
        about how we got here and why

we fantasise our lives
    into what we are not
        because we do not know what we are

it feels good in the moment
    until the moment passes
        and we are adrift again

in the unsettled space between
    our state of being
        and how it will end

Absence

St Patrick's Day, 2020

I hold a shamrock in my hand this St Patrick's Day,
well, that is, I am holding a leafless stem,
as mis-shaped a plant as this mis-shaped world we're in,
so close, yet so distant, so together, so apart.

I long for those three little leaves to bloom, to see
the show-off smiles on three young dressed-up
faces, absent too, this wholly abnormal day.

Travels Back and Forth

I

I think you'll be the best of them, he'd say,
the two of us trudging through oozing mud
on the way from one job to another,
to fix a barbed wire fence in the square field,
then top up barrels in the L-field with water
pumped struggling up the hill from the river below
to fill big rusty mugs for cattle to slake their thirst
and wet their pink sandpaper tongues.

Striding like a man to keep pace with him,
not wanting to let on how hard I had to work
to not get stuck or fall down in the muck,
though now and then my foot moved on
without my little wellington, and he had to
backtrack to rescue it and me.

His words encouraged me and I believed him,
though it might have been his way of getting
the most out of me to better marshal cows
through gaps and gates or stack up bales of hay.
When he offered praise or let me help him do a job
it made me feel sky-tall, the way I might have felt
if he had lifted me up in a hefty hug.

I took comfort, being the last of the litter,
that there was no one to dethrone me.
In the bliss of innocence, the thought
that he might have said the same to the others
never crossed my blinkered mind.

II

Dad was a high fielder and teller of tall tales,
like the one about two men who had to work
for days on end with shovels to mix mustard
for sandwiches, such was the size of the crowd
expected to attend a big rally by the lake.

He could make and mend all kinds of gadgetry
with scraps of metal from bits of old machines
he kept in the open-fronted shed across the yard,
shelves stacked with jars of new and used nails, nuts,
bolts, screws and hinges. However bent and crooked,
he could hammer them into shape to meet the need
of the moment, with the same ingenuity he brought
to the recitations he'd unveil from time to time.

He looked for a bargain in every shop, a discount
for his custom or no deal. As he would say of others
who displayed a wisdom beyond the norm,
he was himself like someone *who was out before*,
this man of many worlds, forecaster, theorist,
expert reader of man, beast, climate and nature,
only child of a long line.

III
He was the go-to man when neighbours needed
help – a tractor to pull a cow out of a drain,
machinery to sow and save crops, his car to take
them to the doctor or to visit friends in hospital,
always on the go and always with his chat on board.

On long drives to boats and planes
I listened to the talk of emigrants on their way
to join relatives, or going lonely to the unknown.
Stories and yarns would bounce around
the car in a game of verbal throw-the-ball
and then a silence, triggered by a memory stirred,
a remembered loss of loved ones left behind
or a flash across the mind of the suppressed reality
that at this journey's end lay the beginning
of the unfamiliar.

He'd be lonely too on the way home
not knowing if they would ever meet again,
me there in the back seat to shorten the journey,
keeping him awake with questions and answers
to questions as he recounted a fair day here,
a job done there, irons in many a fire, stories
of dealing men and fighting men, heroes he had met
or read about, from the Fenians to the Behans,
his hopes for a day when all Ireland would be one,
founding dreams fulfilled.

IV

We worked through endless all-season days
in the fields, stopping only for tea from a can
carried to us by my mother, or buttermilk
from the churn on hot summer days, best swallowed
at speed, like the slippery raw eggs we downed
for strength and energy after football training,
with big batch bread sandwiches of boiled ham,
despatched with a fierce frenzy, like hungry
livestock might devour sparse winter fodder.

We would pause sometimes to settle a dispute
about how best to do the job in hand
or to take stock of clouds on the other side
of the lake, with pretend bets laid as to whether
they would come across, he backing the water
to divert them off track and, as the clouds parted,
keep going boys, he'd say, *we'll have no rain today.*

Days when swallows seemed to fly as high
as planes to forage for their share of food,
we knew it would stay dry. When they
were seen to dive and glide close to the ground
in pursuit of prey on the wing, we understood
the rain was not too far behind and with it
some respite from the back-break of the day,
a chance to play-act under shelter, or practise
throwing rings or darts until it passed.

Match results and politics fed the daily banter,
voices and arms rising with the tempo of debate
that could turn so ferocious as to risk engulfing all,
even Shep the dog felt obliged to scurry off at times,
tail between legs, to cower at a safe distance
until things cooled down. When it sounded in danger
of boiling over, Dad would defuse the situation, saying,
it'll be all the same in a hundred years' time,
let's get this job done lads.

And so it went from season to season,
from job to job, through setting spuds
to saving hay and footing turf, spreading dung
on fledgling crops, filling corn in sacks of jute,
thinning beet, snagging turnips, rounding up
cattle from the football field and the fort field,
where fairy folk were known to cavort by night,
or trimming hedges in the field with furze
in the middle, where rabbits at the grassy edge
darted for cover at my less than furtive approach.

V

Days flew into years and I was soon away.
The world he knew like the back of his hand
was changing. New rich-era roads only served
to lead him astray, drive him to distraction.
Shocking religious revelations and unholy
political liaisons increased his feeling of unease.
Landscapes of familiarity shifting and evolving
into unfamiliar, yet undeniable, new orders.
Above all, the loss of his lifetime's crop of love
heralded a harvest of harsh decline.

On a visit home from abroad in the final weeks,
I saw in his face a reflection of the reality
that some of his certainties were open to question,
turning the past into a precarious present
and a fearful future. Illness had him in its vice grip
and search as we might, there was no bit on his shelf
that could fix this faltering engine.

We talked about the journey he had travelled,
the twists and scrapes we shared along the way.
Though our paths diverged in the years between,
I still believed in him as in those far-off formative
days and told him so. We hugged. This time
it was for real. And as we parted, we spoke about
my coming back for good. It would be very soon.
In the end, soon was to prove too late.

Dancers

Sometimes they danced
the whole night through
not noticing the sun had set,
its fire still burning in their hearts,
its heat a brand upon their brains;
the songs, the poems, the love
they shared with wine
till stars gave way to dawn,
the soundtrack of the decades saved
to be replayed, long after,
when the heat is gone,
the dancing done.

Reading the Sundays

After Sunday dinner (in the middle
of the day) they retreated to their regular
chairs to read the Sunday papers,
the *Sunday Independent* and *Sunday Review*.
Later the *Sunday World*, *Press* and *Tribune*
all became part of the mix.

As with the dailies, Dad's first focus
fell on the death notices, *to make sure
I'm not among them* he would joke
while noting funerals to be attended,
before proclaiming, *there are people
dying today who never died before.*

Calling out snippets to each other
from various articles, their tone
of voice revealing whether the item
found favour or was being frowned upon;
the source usually informed the tone,
the more *official*, the greater the scorn.

Sections were swapped over
as each was read until the papers
were fully exchanged, their order
re-arranged and some parts discarded
in keeping with my parents' interpretation
of the news and articles therein.

Dozing off mid-read was part of the ritual,
pages crumpling like rumpled blankets
on their laps or hanging sideways
half on the ground in a disordered tousle.
This was their day of rest unless something
of a higher order pressed itself onto the agenda.

Some sunny Sundays, Mam converted the car
in the yard into her personal conservatory
to finish the papers and grab a peaceful nap
while Dad lay back in his chair snoring
and dreaming that his much wished-for
six-day-cow had at last come to pass.

A Game of Two Halves

That man Packie Bonner should be canonised
you declared, when you phoned
the day after Ireland beat England
in Stuttgart at Euro 88.

It was the first time I can remember that you
had ever mentioned soccer or taken
any interest in the foreign game,
so it came as a surprise.

I waited for the declaration of Packie's deification
after his dramatic penalty shoot-out save
against Romania in Genoa
that famous Italia '90 day.

You didn't phone. Perhaps your interest in the game
had waned, Mam; or more likely your interest
in the opposition wasn't quite
the same this time round.

Still, the night before you passed you asked
when I called if I was in Seville where Ireland
was playing Spain in the next
world cup campaign.

You had seen a friend of mine in the crowd on TV
and knew we had been at matches together
in Germany for the Europeans
and Italy for the World Cup.

I wasn't in Spain that night and though the glory days
for Jack and the squad continued to USA '94
and beyond, everything since Seville
has been played in added time.

August

The harvest sun is high,
warm without a breeze.
It would be a great day
for the fields, to be listening
to your yarns break the weight of work
at this gathering-in time.

There might even be mention
of your birthday, though seldom
was it marked in a crowded family
birthday month, last year an exception
for your four score.

Instead, we are gathered in cold quiet
listening to orations about your life,
your number eight club jersey displayed,
its green and gold mirroring the glistening
tricolour, as the speakers sketch your prowess
on and off the pitch, rooted in the traditions
of our games and the republican culture
you cherished as a direct inheritance
from the leaders of the Rising.

The many episodes and anecdotes
laid out before the congregation
jog our whisperings,
massage our grief.

Flashback

for Luke

Which one? asked my mother
as her teacher eyes studied a photo
of two lads in a busy street scene.

I'd told her I had befriended
a son of her school inspector
and that he was in the picture.

The street photographer had caught
the two of us in glorious monochrome
crossing Dublin's O'Connell Bridge,

striding out on a sunny Saturday
afternoon, faces full of destination
shadows sideways on the pavement.

It is not that I was dishevelled
in that snapshot decades ago,
it was my rapid transition

from shy rural school-going teen
to free-roving man about town
that caught her a moment off guard.

Would she recognise me now —
twenty years older than she was then?
Do we recognise each other from those

headier days with our shades and shapes
before we morphed through versions
of ourselves to become ourselves?

Journey

for Ellen
(missing since 3 November, 1999)

I see you still
all bouncy and beautiful,
a total city girl, wild
in the wide fields
of a fertile farm,
stumped by the discovery
that milk did not come
pre-packed from cows.

I meet you
decades later, a woman
in your own urban space,
innocence long gone,
trying to grind sense
out of reality.

I think of you
alone, leaving for home,
your heart limp with loss
for your mother passed
and sister left behind,
as you departed for the boat
from Holyhead to Dublin.

I wonder who
was the last to talk
to you. Did you chat about
your journey, your love
of family, music, your love
of life, the things
you planned to do
when you got home?

Roll Call

A bird atop a tree keeps sharp lookout,
a jackdaw or a crow, it's hard to tell
against the glare the sun has spread about,
its feathers flutter in a breezy swell.
Lithe blue tits dart from branch to fence to hedge;
alert to dangers posed by prowling cat,
they chirp shrill warnings from a safer ledge.
A robin drops in silence from a slat,
an unsuspecting insect in its sights.
Each piece of nature's puzzle finds its place.
When daily bustle settles into nights
we gather all our own for safe embrace,
aware that unexpected tolls may sound,
we pray our fragile pieces are all found.

Harvesting
for Eimear (2020)

The tree of time grows fruit for every season,
a source to feed the soul if other crops should fail.

In every leaf a tune that dances on the branch,
a memory afloat inside each budding note.

Kernels found when outer shells crack open
reveal a core that spreads a honeyed glow

to ears that pause to hear the melodies
of magic handed down, and freshly honed

across the years of picking up on clues
orchestrated in a string of different ways.

A Peter Skellern song on radio in 2019 rewinds
three decades to a night of Suppressed Songsters

when, as special guest in Horta's Palais des Beaux-Arts,
he performed 'You're a Lady' and other classics.

You were singing that night, learning the violin too,
and we were learning to stop calling it a fiddle.

In truth it was both and more, a door opened
to a world of scores and trads, and so it remains.

Strains of Malcolm Arnold's 'March' came wafting
from the open windows of a music room

on sunny afternoons, with John Sheehan's waltz,
gliding in from far Marino, picked up note by note.

Escher's art joined the mix upon your crowded palette,
and with Clann Lir, more than a band was born.

Soon you were out the door to hit a trail of stages,
pits and festivals from Scandinavia to Provence.

In fair Granada, a year of study led to lock-in nights
in Barcelona bars and back to Bewley's Oriental Café.

Bands of Lazy Dawgs rolled round like tumbleweed
by night, while hard-nosed daytime deals were done

to seal the bread and butter branch that flourished
with the rest in your creative cocktail of success,

still growing, nourishing your own crop as you go.
Before you knew it, you were rocking up

with your first-born to a Taylor Swift stadium gig,
like I did with you for Roxette's Joyride Tour in '92.

So many memories made through all the seasons,
harvested for recall at times like these.

summer song

let's not squander

the stronger light
of longer days

let's harvest it

with honey, nuts,
most precious crop

let's gather in

the warm flavour
before it fades

let's savour all

it has to give
each luscious drop

Learning to Swim

After a hot dusty day in the hayfield
we would go for a dip in the lake.

Never a swim.
Full of bog holes, my father warned,
strong men had drowned there,
men with heroic deeds to their names
could not be saved.

Fear fully formed,
stuck in the shallows for decades,
it took a sizzling Greek islands holiday
and the lure of the welcoming
Aegean to spur me on.

Back in Dublin,
determined to be brave, I misjudged
a grab for the side and went under
at the deep end, nearly drowning
in my panic to survive.

It was this mishap
that gave me the final push
and the courage to believe I could dive
into the deep, with nothing but water
for support, and keep going.

When I drift back to that bog-holed lake
I wonder if I have ever fully let go.

Lightning Strike

We scram for cover
to hide under the stairs,
the furthest point from windows
and doors, to be safe from the lightning,
the darkest place in the house,
as futile as trying to catch
a fistful of wind.

We count the number
of seconds between the flash
and the somersaulting crescendo
of the thunder clap to calculate
the distance, a mile for every second,
separating us from the spot
where the lightning struck.

*The man above rolling
barrels again*, my father quips
to allay our fears, as we sit at the table
looking up at JFK and Pádraig Pearse
while the Sacred Heart, with its
ever-red lightning spark,
has our backs.

We laugh but we know the danger
is real – haven't we been told
often enough about how, years ago,
lightning struck the front window,
its blast mark still plain to see
like a surgeon's incision
that has never fully healed.

moments

today I watched a squirrel
watching me
the two of us attracted
to a tree
it is a truly wondrous
thing to be
together in such moments
roaming free

Awaiting News
for M

The postman brings me no more letters
like the wild ones you once wrote
about your exploits in America,
the madness of attending to the cares
of rich and fun-loving ladies,
your lonely soul full of poetry
and you longing for a feed of porter.

Mad nights with you back in Dublin,
sessions in O'Donoghue's, Toners,
Mulligan's and McDaids fuelling
late-night banter in Mrs Gaj's.
Politics, poetry, philosophy discussed
with gusto amid a flood of porter
so high it could have drowned us both.

You headed out of town again
to shake off the stress of city ways
and live a pilgrim kind of life
on a remote west coast island,
in search of a better, truer, state.
I too moved from place to place
as we drifted on our separated tides.

You surfaced from the dark, years later,
a headline on the early morning news —
overnight, a dinghy hit rough waves,
occupants tossed into the Atlantic.
Known locally to be a strong swimmer,
you were named as the only one
to make it safely to the shore.

The report described you as a fisherman.
To me you were a hunter, a pusher
of boundaries, chasing deep and wide,
swimming against currents while others
sheltered along the shore. With all you have
hooked and hauled across the years,
I hope you have also caught your truth.

Nocturne

Seen through gin-drenched eyes,
the tear-stained moon looks lonely on its own.

The playlist shuffles from Waits to Cohen.
If this late-night contemplation was lightened
by your presence and the promise of sweet everythings,
how much better it would be for the full round moon and me.

A blob of cloud intrudes and in the shadow that it casts,
I reach out for the bottle and pour another glass.

From Notes made at Camden Lock
for Caroline (2022)

I found the poems I wrote for you
when you were nine and heading off
with your classmates for company
on your first big trip away from home.

A rhyme a day from Monday to Friday,
silly lines I hoped you'd find funny,
a joke of the day too in case
my bardic effort to amuse fell short.

Maybe I should have given you
puzzles and problems to solve instead,
though you might have found
my attempts at those even more absurd.

You probably made your own calculations
as to how far you were from home
and how long it would take to get back
by the legally allowed motorway limits.

But you stuck with the skill-learning,
swimming at speed with different strokes.
On a later outing you took to the slopes, the first
of many peaks you would target and reach.

Home then was Belgium where all roads
led to another country. We revelled
in the opportunity for travel and adventure
sightseeing our way across the continent.

On a day-long drive south we had sausage
for breakfast in Germany, lunchtime sandwiches
of cheese and Irish crisps in Switzerland,
before stopping for dinner the far side of Venice.

We feasted *al fresco* on pasta and pizza
followed by the *pièce de résistance* –
giant gelati topped with Cadbury's chocolate
still solid from the cool box in the boot.

You would ask me to tell you stories
from my schooldays, dodging haircuts, midnight
feasts and other illicit activities, my days and nights
ruled by summoning bells and summary punishments.

Your own school years and achievements
notched up fast and soon our marathon
road trips were no match as you took off
on your more exotic far-flung forays.

Such are some scattered nuggets of memory
that come into focus as I make notes at Camden Lock
watching for you to come through the throng
surrounding the maze of market stalls below.

The low March sun stunts my gaze, glints off
my near-enough-to-lunchtime beer; you appear
from behind, coffee in hand, surprising me as with
this trip, a surprise for your mother's birthday.

I listen to the story of your day so far,
the dress you nearly bought, the bag you want
to go back to look at and likely buy
before we head off to meet her for lunch.

I store this moment in my pocket notebook
to preserve it as a future memory or maybe a poem
noting as I do how you have become a storyteller
to me and how wonderful that makes me feel.

From other notebooks I draw memories
of shared visits to New York, Madrid, Vienna
and many more with you as our guide and provider
of ideas for activities to pursue, places to unwind.

The world's highest hands-free skywalk is not
the only height you have scaled as you plotted a way
up your chosen path; lately you've begun to hit
key notes in a throwback to your musical youth.

It took a pandemic to scupper your grand plan
for trans-world travel. I sense the loss of stories
you would have told on your return but cherish
even more the journeys we make together.

made to last

we walk together in the park
and talk about the weather

noting how the days are growing
shorter darker colder wetter

then we talk of making art
how most of it is made to last

unlike those longer brighter days
whose colour drains away so fast

Moving On

I am upstream east of Heidelberg
on the scenic Neckar when it comes to me
with more clarity than ever before:
I am more than what others demand of me.
The moment is hammered into the chain
that links memory to circumstance.

Time to put an end to the endless chasing
and second-guessing of diverse positions,
to be written up in briefings, on the myriad
of pros & cons of one policy position over
another. Time to file away the files. Time to
make my words my own and let them flow.

The late May air is warm, beer ice cold,
the cruise boat burps along in lazy chugs,
steep-sided banks of evergreens and vines
float past. I lean back like a sunflower
face to the sun and invite the future
to sweep me into its slipstream.

Déjà vu

Don't go back, they said,
go forward, and I did, forward
to the streets I used to know so well,
where pity is seldom sought
but often given.

I traipse to places once familiar
some the same, some reborn
baby-new, some without trace
except for ghosts that shift uneasily
on high stools long displaced.

On Harry Street, Phil Lynott stands,
his commanding gaze engaging all
in the heart of his old town. I move on,
recalling moments of poetry and pints
once shared upon our high-stool stage.

In basement bars bursting with words
waves of familiar odours waft through,
a new generation discovers the thrill
of limitless creativity and uncovers
the wealth embedded in what went before.

To my surprise, I fit in with ease
to conversations on the old order,
the new order and the disorder,
hearts and arms open to embrace
a wanderer returning to his trade.

Poets not long born inhabit corners
mixing rhymes with songwriter souls,
combining to create their own anthems
telling it like it is, like it was
and like it will be again.

In a haze of past thought, I leave behind
the hum of the new to make my way home,
taking comfort in the glow of knowing
that in this strange uncertain world
some things remain intent on being true.

Whispers

I can only speak of what is in me,
the rest I must assemble and diffuse.

A blackbird parks and fills me with its song,
bright daffodils push back the darker shades,
great oak trees sift the air to let me breathe,
fresh dew relieves my early morning thirst.
All these the seeds for thoughts that form the words
I mould and whisper to the breeze which wafts
them off to places out of reach, to seep
through sand into the depths of seas and rise
to rest upon a fertile beach, and there
take root to bloom anew, sweet food for bees.

I scatter thoughts in words to spread afar
like stars send light to whisper to the night.

Lines

I was searching for a line I found first lines and last lines front lines and back lines long lines short lines thin lines broad lines narrow lines broken lines unbroken lines fine lines soft lines guidelines bylines timelines deadlines straplines outlines headlines hairlines eyelines neck lines face lines age lines laugh lines jawlines bra lines bustlines hem lines visible lines panty lines pralines waist lines worry lines lifelines live lines chat lines datelines breadlines break-up lines blood lines family lines fashion lines clotheslines hanging out to dry lines highlines coke lines doing lines adrenalines goal lines sidelines touchlines starting lines finishing lines fishing lines trampolines zip lines disciplines indisciplines assembly lines parade lines boundary lines border lines attack lines battle lines enemy lines defensive lines fault lines behind the lines demarcation lines baselines firing lines lines in the sand lines beelines draglines imaginary lines inclines declines reclines flatlines guy-lines tie-lines vaselines opening lines hard lines streamlines parallel lines horizontal lines rooflines skylines tree lines sightlines horizon lines coastlines water lines white lines yellow lines green lines red lines bluelines blurred lines quinolines walking the white lines straight lines crooked lines standing in lines phone lines helplines holding lines direct lines landlines extension lines onlines offlines taglines busy lines cross lines dropping lines lines of communication hotlines ah-here-now lines connecting lines power lines pipelines transmission lines traffic lines airlines bus lines tramlines train lines branch lines main lines changing lines circle lines suburban lines old lines end of the line lines brake lines snail lines cruise lines ferry lines shipping lines shorelines new lines latitude lines longitude lines lines of business supply lines credit lines production lines top lines bottom lines extended lines sales lines picket lines closing lines lines of enquiry along the lines dotted lines sticking to lines well-worn lines underlines drawing lines tracing lines tossing lines saying lines suggested lines subject lines between the lines carolines mandolines song lines writing lines poetry lines lines written on a seat on the grand canal dublin lines written in early spring lines written a few miles above tintern abbey forgetting lines write it out a hundred times lines remembering my lines plot lines fluffing my lines winning lines felines masculines punch lines I am searching for a line I have found all kinds of lines twenty-seven lines of lines not my lines

end lines

Undelivered

Flowers in a pretty bunch,
left behind upon a bench.

A bouquet full of smiling scent.
Forgotten or forsaken?

Longshots
for Alison

We meet in the lounge
of the local, less noisy mid-morning
than the café next door.

At the bar,
punters pick plausible propositions,
pausing sips of early morning pints
to place bets in the bookies upstairs.
They know the day will breed
frustration more than celebration.
They ignore the science of experience
for the compensation of the chance
to beat the odds.

On the other side, we are
poetry partners picking pronouns
and prepositions to fit the lines,
mine and hers going neck and neck
towards some illusory finishing post –
a book against all odds or mere crumpled pages
in the wastepaper pile of also rans.
The going can be good at times, heavy at others,
mostly fair to middling.

We race along together
in pursuit of precarious projects.
Whether crafted with skill or stumbled
upon by chance, the rare success
of a winning formula breaking the line
at just the right time, renders the chase
worth the while.

A Bit of Bad Language

for Saoirse & Colm

There's a little bit of bad language,
whispers the front of house attendant
as she checks my ticket on the way into
the production of a play written by a friend.

(I wonder who else received this subtle caution).

On my way out from an engaging performance
I see the attendant in conversation by the bar,
there's an awful lot of good language too,
I whisper as I pass.

The Reading and the Recital

The Steinway is sideways and so am I.
The final programme running order
arranged as the invited audience arrives
for a cultural soirée of words and music
in the Embassy of Ireland.

Introductions diplomatically done,
first the poet and then the celebrated pianist.
Mouth dry from a mix of June Parisian heat
and a fast-beating pulse urging me to leave.
No turning back now.

The expectant audience fans out in arc formation,
the ornateness of the room more imposing
than the nearby Arc de Triomphe.
Chat subsides. Silence rises.
The pianist prepares to press the keys.

Brahms's 'Capriccio' sets a lively start.
I urge my words to match the precision of the notes,
a lullaby to a lost future.
The music takes over as O'Carolan's
haunting final composition lulls us with its beauty.

My footprints catch dust,
smoke without fire in a changing light.
A Schubert 'Impromptu' sits us up straight.
Intermezzo. The poet speaks of encounters with love
and night owls in woods to the north.

The 'Hungarian Dance No 1' takes us
trickling through the warm evening to a calm finale.
The maestro raises his hands. Applause fills the space.
The performers are recalled to take the acclaim
and mingle with guests taking canapés and wine.

When it dawns over Paris and me,
I saunter down to the Seine, view the queue
outside Notre Dame, take coffee by the window
in Shakespeare & Co., sit still for a moment,
release myself into the rhythm of the day.

In-Betweenness

(from work created for the ArtNetdlr Hinterland Collaborative Project, 2019)

for Hilary

Cold stones by the beach capture a glint of evening light,
momentary blossoms on a monotone sandscape.

After we ran aground we found new headlands,
dilapidated paths led us through a blur of briary furze
to open marshes, fertile wetlands, refuge for wild life.

Tree trunks skulk by the marsh's edge, bare broken branches
crane to watch us pass, protruding roots, wrapped serpent-like around
each other, threaten our progress.

A man at the edge relieves himself, adding to the detritus.
Further in, the shapes of mountains, stained by winter's
harshest frost and sun-dried rains of summer, slope down
to meet the woods above the new roads straddling the outer scatter.

In between, the hubbub of the hinterland, sinews stretched
with every breath. Remnants of salt marsh, sanctuary for species of wildlife
to rest and refuel among flowers, shrubs, weathered plants.

Circles of green in brackish water, graceful flight of the heron,
its harsh call of arrival a siren for the hard lives of those
who come here to sleep and leave behind relics of their presence
to taunt our consciences;

flutter of its swift wings before the splish as water is sliced
with precision. Squawks and sweeter chirps from hedges
and tangled growth, over which hawks stalk their prey, screech
of wheels on steel of rail line dividing marsh from sea.

Small boats bob, stiff breeze drives clouds to blow shimmering showers in
over the brown shore, across the space inside where news once went back
and forth in written words, images unseen, linking people and places.

Flying ships now criss-cross above this space that harbours history
from before the city spread its cloak to wrap around a hinterland
of plenty, rising to the hills, sheltered by mountains,
slanting to the sea, sinking in the swamp of progress,

ever-changing, evolving within its own skin,
open to the world, orbiting on its axis while generations
spin past, each believing they have seen the best of it.

We find our own hinterland in the space between the image
and the reality of place. Our past and future bound by nature
as the railway binds city to suburb and beyond.

Like migrant species and sanctuary seekers,
we too must move on.

Wintering

Pale winter sun creeps low across bare quiet fields,
a wave of biting wind whips through near naked trees,
the brighter sounds of summer long since switched to mute,
from ditch-to-ditch slink stealthy shapes in search of food.

Words on the Street

She writes on the street, it passes the time
and catches the eye of some passers-by.
She smiles when a child drops coins on her mat.
Marketing lads on their big pedal cars
weave up and down through the Saturday crowds
touting the chance of a big lotto win.

Shoppers with bargains and satisfied smiles
rub shoulders with punters in search of fun.
Some walk on her chalk not seeing the words
or pause for selfies to capture the mood.
She knows not all can commit to her cause
so many must carry cares of their own.

Know her by name, know the shame of her plight.
She writes how she feels down there on her knees
on this Grafton Street patch she inhabits.
At end of day when flower sellers take
the colours away she feels more alone
and wishes she too could pack to go home.

She wraps her chalk up and gathers her hope.
Tonight she will sleep however she can
and wake to recall the words that she wrote
to tell passers-by she *could use helping
hands, that being homeless she can't afford
to be shy*. Then she'll go and start over.

Outsiders

They came with stories of the war,
and battles that would set them free,
to land upon a friendly shore.
They came with stories of the war.
Shattered by all our shuttered doors,
dangerous as the darkest sea,
they came with stories of the war
and battles that would set them free.

Direct Knowledge

It is said
we should have known
but mostly we didn't
because we did not
have the knowledge
to know that things were
other than they seemed,
other than we were told
to believe.

It took decades
and tribunals of inquiry
to reveal truths,
extract apologies, promises of
no repeats.

Now we have the knowledge
to know that some things
seem other than they ought to be.

In another future
it may be asked again
why we did not act.

ask

if you don't know

ask those who have no money
ask those who have no home
ask those who have no jobs
ask those who had to leave
ask those who had to flee
ask those with no voice
ask the money-makers
ask all the politicians
ask opinion shapers
ask civil servants
ask the teachers
ask the clerics
ask the street
ask yourself

ask

Lullaby to a Lost Future

November, 2016

The sudden thud of darkness falling down
impacted like a punch, a big ka-pow,
as in some comic strip; who's laughing now?
This darkness shrouds another kind of clown.

A poet picked this moment to depart
he left us his vision of disorder
said he'd seen the future, it was murder.
We wonder now what Leonard meant. The start

of time when freedoms will be put on hold,
a portent of a deadly darker age?
Blue light projected on an empty stage,
plain truths denied by lies that will enfold

and gather like a poison to be puked.
But beauty still will flourish in the roots
of trees no longer free to bear new fruits.
All those who live for flowers, when rebuked,

in search of sleep will count each petalled bloom
and dream of landscapes only they can see,
great landscapes where again they will be free
to hold a light to shift this heavy gloom.

The Morning After
November, 2020

This early Sunday morning is bright and quiet.
Bare trees open a clear view from my upstairs window.
Across the street, all I expect to see within my frame
of vision is in its place – houses, gardens, hedges,
windows dressed in curtains, some still closed,
driveways housing family cars in front of doors
behind which other lives go on.

What I see could be a still life scene.
A sight that for a moment causes me to shiver
when I think how, in a flash, it all could change,
this snapshot of a tranquil moment at a time and place
that will never be repeated, as the leaf that fell
onto the path just now will never fall again.

This thought is superseded by the calmer one
that after every winter, comes a spring.

Transformed

It starts
with the seep
of a tender trickle
before the gurgle of sound
filters down, cool, clear and clean
it creeps away from its earthy cradle,
gathers great strength as it grows to a stream
and strides along to swell the veins that give us life,
the rolling river crashes into the dam of human progress.
Distressed, it emerges from a tip head babble of formulas
and indifferences to foam away in scientific fumes,
its natural features contaminated and changed,
many of its living creatures destroyed,
rearranged, a carrier of disease
expanding to attack the land,
choking all it overlaps,
an agent of death
itself slowly
dying

In a Spin

The sea whispers to the shore
there are no words, no words anymore.
It confides to the sand that it is choking
in a strangle of stacked up packaging.
Everything backing up,
stifled outlets forced to reverse their flow,
water and waste push back to their base.
Sinks and toilets jammed-up and stinking
overflow onto streets, across fields, down roads,
filling rivers and lakes as they squeeze a last gasp
from their plasticated lungs
before everything spins way out of control.
There are no words, no words anymore.

Surge

I hear the water foaming
beyond the cold cold mountain

it froths a rising murmur
of a stormy surge to come

a thunder of emotion
builds deep beneath the surface

we trundle towards disaster
in a blur of damning news

frustrated by allegiance
to the leadership of some

deniers of the science
and the truth it has defined

I hear the water roaring
in the anguish of a child

I sense the mountain coming
while we scramble final words

Storm Warning

When we were walking once amid a storm
you told me that when trees begin to fall
the safest place to run to is the trunk.
I love that you're my safe place. When it's dark,
your bark enfolds me in protective wrap.

Sometimes you are my bite against attack,
I love you for that too and when it's calm
I love to play at being a weatherman,
predicting dire storms, wild and angry winds
that send me running to my safest berth
to which I cling until the force subsides.
In windless peace we settle down to sleep.

I love you when on unexpected days
you, too, pretend a storm is on its way.

Christmas Craic

When lights come down
when tinsel's gone
there may be cracks
where there were none.

Let the New Light In

Pull back the curtain
let in the new light,
pack the dark winter
away out of sight.

Let new thoughts blossom
and grow to full bloom,
out with the old ones
that darkened the room

Sing a new anthem
let music hold sway,
with poems full of hope
begin each new day.

Ring bells raise a cheer
let laughter be loud,
lift minds to the sky
disperse the dark cloud.

Make love make it last
dance life round the floor,
spring has come knocking
fling open the door.

Victory Flight

a wedge of geese
    in perfect flight formation
        carves its way arrow-like through the evening sky
    I ask if you have seen them
you tell me no

but that you heard
    their plaintive cries,
        you tell me you admire their uncompromising
    determination to make it
to their destination

you grab hold of me
    my feet tread the air
        I coast at ease in your trail, our flight path
    carved between moon and stars
we make landfall

This is a day the dead would like

a heart-lift day of hope and light.
A flush of heat from sudden sun
and out we stream for chat-filled fun
as birds through hedges flirt and flit
announcing with excited zest
their readiness to love and nest,
fleet starling and the loud blue tit.

The raucous caws of circling crows
sound oddly more melodious,
amid the hum that gathers pace
the shrieks of gulls on scavenge chase
seem less a threat or none at all.
Wild laughter sprays from garden swings
across the green a soft breeze brings
percussive beat of bouncing ball.

In longer grass wild flowers thrive
while insect life brings earth alive,
fresh buttercups and daisies beam
and down along the spring-filled stream
the wood's awash with bluebell haze;
a bee sets down to catch its breath
then hovers off good news to spread.
It's one of those most treasured days

when all the species are aligned
and everything's begun to grow,
a turning day my friends would like
but one that they will never know.

All You Can Do

If you are open to it, let yourself
amaze your heart with all that you can do,

you may not see stars in a daylit stream
or find your fortune at a rainbow's end

the sun may not break through the cloud and rain
or embers shield you from deep winter cold,

but free yourself to share the things you know
to learn your neighbour's ways and show respect

enrich the lives of others with your smile
keep up a steady beat behind the noise

know that the further down young roots take hold
the richer they will flourish when they grow,

let not the scales of others block your view –
be open and the way will lead you through.

Core Value

Pare back to the core and then more,
remove the silk and satin layers
reveal the bare within
feel the dips
and curves
the texture of the velvet
and the rough, observe each blemish,
talk about the odd bits, the shapes that do not fit,
spare no blush, disabuse yourself of the notion of perfection,
rejoice in all you have laid out and learned. Here you will find
where to begin.

Running

I am running in my shadow
I am trying to catch my breath
my shadow is growing longer
I must be taking shorter steps.

overheard by trees

the trees are full
    of all they hear these days
roots deep-processing
    what it means where it fits
they whisper to each other
    in the language of their trade

the things the children say
    the games they play with gusto
the lusty talk of lovers
    as they make their way to work
or stroll out after dinner
    and pause to lean against a trunk

the complaining tone of workers
    in dispute with boss or brother
the conniving plans of plotters
    who walk in circles as they talk
others cannot say what impulse
    makes them kick at trunks in anger

the trees shiver their leaves
    and I swear I hear them murmur
to each other as I pass
    with all that they have witnessed
in so many years of growing
    the likes of this they have not known

the thing that has them boggled
    is not the flood of strange new words
but the manner of the utterances
    like never heard and in their roots
they fear decay will eat their souls
    I lean in close and sotto voce say *I know*

Night Shift

They fold into each other's parts
together in the quiet dark
like flowers closing on themselves
against the predators of night,
to open out with stronger hearts
to brighten garden, field and park;
like dusty books upon the shelves
their covers keeping pages white,
they bask in touch of flesh on flesh
till sleep enfolds them in its mesh.

ups & downs

mothers and fathers
sitting in pubs

remembering nights
they danced in clubs

their sons and daughters
out on the town

some growing up
some slowing down

Footage

Take me to the snow
      so I can r
              o
                l
                  l
    in it before it goes
    so I can go with it
    and when they show
    the footage
you will see me
flashing past the lens
so   fast
you will have

                d
             n
           i
        w
     e
to   r

many times
before you can

freeze frame me.

Now go back

frame
     by
          frame

along the track I've made,
see the shape
I've left
behind.

Fast forward.

In the Middle of the Woods

i.m. Nuala Finnegan

In the middle of the woods
raindrops hang in knuckles
from bare bony branches
before they buckle under the swell
and drop in twisted patterns
to sunder away in streams
searching for a river.

There is a silence to the rain
from our warm vantage
inside the wall-length window.
We are gathered to work with our words
willing them to swell and drop and flow,
twelve hands at work together,
apostles writing future gospels.

Every drop must do its job
to navigate hurdles seen and hidden,
some make it to the river
some never get beyond the fall
but all are here and real and now,
as real as every breath we make
before we break for food
and chat about the this and that
of lives well lived in our own ways,
filling in our family frames,
regaling with more familiar tales
of artistic paths traversed
before the one that brought us
to sit around this table.

When our host turns talk
to the sport of kings, my mind
runs ahead to thoughts of success.
Filled with the zest of our musings,
notions of failing or falling are
non-runners as we clink our glasses
in unspoken celebration of ourselves.

kindling

set a fire
strike a match
when it catches
fan the flames
let it burn
spread the ashes
gather twigs
start again

Notes

"In-Betweenness" (page 61):

The poem "In-Betweenness" is an abridged version of work created for the Hinterland Collaborative Project, 2019 organised by ArtNetdlr, a voluntary group of professional artists of every discipline connected to Dun Laoghaire-Rathdown. The poem was part of a poem-film in collaboration with multi-media artist Hilary Williams (with film editing by Bob Gallagher).

The theme for the project was the Hinterland of Dun Laoghaire-Rathdown. Over 50 artists working in various groups took part. The collaborative project is a biennial event for ArtNet. Artists of different disciplines, painters, sculptors, ceramicists, graphic artists, writers, poets, weavers, photographers, animators, filmmakers and composers worked together. The project started in January 2018 and an exhibition of the works created was held in May 2019.

Acknowledgements

Some of the poems in this collection, or versions of them, have previously appeared in: *The Stony Thursday Book; CAPS Poetry Anthology* (2024); *Flare; Skylight 47; The Honest Ulsterman; Live Encounters Poetry; The Storms Issue III; Not The Time To Be Silent* (Collected Work); *UCD Poetry in Lockdown: a Pandemic Archive; Pendemic; The Music of what Happens; Lime Square Poets* (online); *Drawn to the Light Press; Vox Galvia; Decameron* (online); *Bray Arts Journal; Silver Apples Magazine*. Sincere thanks to the editors and publishers concerned for including my poems in their publications.

The poem "overheard by trees" was included in an art exhibition, the theme of which was 'Conversations with Trees' under the auspices of ArtNetdlr (https://artnetdlr.ie/) from December 2023 to March 2024.

The poem "In-Betweenness" is an abridged version of work included in a poem-film created in collaboration with multi-media artist Hilary Williams (with film editing by Bob Gallagher) as part of the Hinterland Collaborative Project, 2019 and associated public exhibition organised by ArtNetdlr. The video of the full piece can be found at https://www.youtube.com/@phillynch2311

My appreciation also to the judges of various poetry competitions in which some of the poems in this collection have been runners-up, highly commended or shortlisted.

Many of the poems were workshopped in writers groups and workshops, particularly in the Dalkey Writers Workshop (DWW) and the 'Lord Edward Group' with special appreciation to my fellow writers, current and former, in both groups. These include Alma Brayden, Ronan Browne, Kevin Burns, Eileen Counihan, Claire Doyle, Andrew Furlong RIP, Mary Hanlon, Phillip Hermann, Miriam Hurley, Robert Kelly, Críona Ní Gháirbhith, Muiris Ó Céidigh, Deryck Payne, Madeline Stringer, Lisa Wixted and other former members of DWW; and from the Lord Edward Group: Peter Clarke, Kevin Conroy, Bernie Crawford, Fiona Fahey, Pauline Flynn, Anne Leahy, Michael Ryan, and Grace Wilentz.

My thanks also to Alison Hackett for her critical contributions during our poetry sparring sessions at which some of the poems were put through their paces. Individual poems were critiqued in various once-off workshops and courses and I'm grateful to all the facilitators and participants for their feedback.

A truly heartfelt thanks to Anne Tannam and Colm Keegan for taking the time to read my manuscript at a number of stages in its evolution and for their valued, insightful and honest feedback as well as for their support and encouragement. My thanks also to Nessa O'Mahony for her feedback on an earlier draft that included versions of many of the poems in this collection. Thanks to Jim Lynch for his careful scrutiny of and feedback on the manuscript text and to Sean Lynch for his feedback on some of the poems in the collection. Thanks also to Amanda Bell for her expert copy-editing of the manuscript.

My thanks and appreciation to Elaine Feeney, Anne Tannam and Colm Keegan for their kind words about the collection.

A special word of deep love and grateful thanks to my family for their help, advice, encouragement, and constant support.

To everyone who inspired, encouraged and facilitated the writing and performance of poems in this collection, including the hosts and audiences of poetry and spoken word events and festivals that have welcomed me and my work to their stages and places around Ireland and further afield, and the many members of the wider poetry and spoken word community that embraced and encouraged me in many ways over the years, thank you all.

And finally, massive thanks and appreciation to Jessie Lendennie and Siobhán Hutson at Salmon Poetry for giving these poems a home where everyone can visit them.

PHIL LYNCH was born in Westmeath and currently lives in Dublin. He also lived in Belgium for several years. His poems have appeared in a wide range of print and online literary journals and anthologies. His work has been featured on national and local radio in Ireland including *Arena, The Poetry Programme, Sunday Miscellany* and 'The Doc on One' on RTE Radio 1; Rhyme & Reason on Dublin South FM and on The Celtic Show broadcast out of Atlanta in the USA. Podcasts in which he has been featured include: *Words Lightly Spoken, Boundless & Bare* and *Eat the Storms*. Some of his poems and adaptations of others have been recorded on CDs. He has been a winner, runner up and highly commended finalist in various poetry competitions.

His previous poetry collection, *In a Changing Light*, was published by Salmon Poetry in 2016. He is a regular reader of his work at poetry and spoken word events and festivals in Ireland (including Electric Picnic Festival, Bray Literary Festival, Dublin Book Festival, Cuirt Literary Festival (Spoken Word Platform), Blackwater International Poetry Festival, Red Line Book Festival, St Patrick's Festival, Dublin: A Year in Words – Poetry & Spoken Word Trail) and has performed at events in Paris, Brussels, London, New York and Washington.

Phil is a coordinator and sometimes host of the *Words by the Sea* monthly event in Dun Laoghaire under the auspices of ArtNetdlr. He was a member of the organising committee for the Bray Literary Festival 2019-2022 and a co-founder and board member of the LINGO Spoken Word Festival (2014-2016). He is a professional member of the Irish Writers Centre, a member of ArtNetdlr (Artist Network Dun Laoghaire-Rathdown), a member of Dalkey Writers Workshop and the 'Lord Edward' writing group.

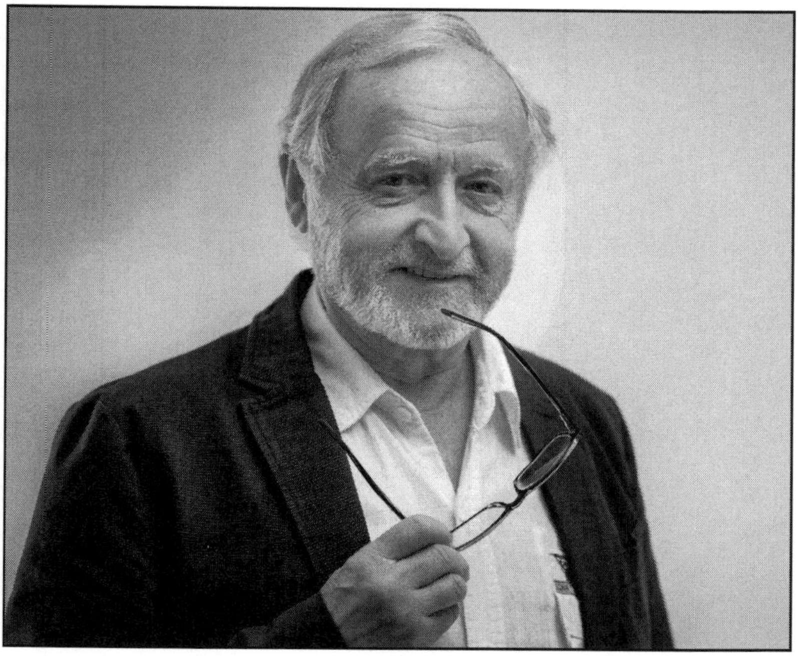

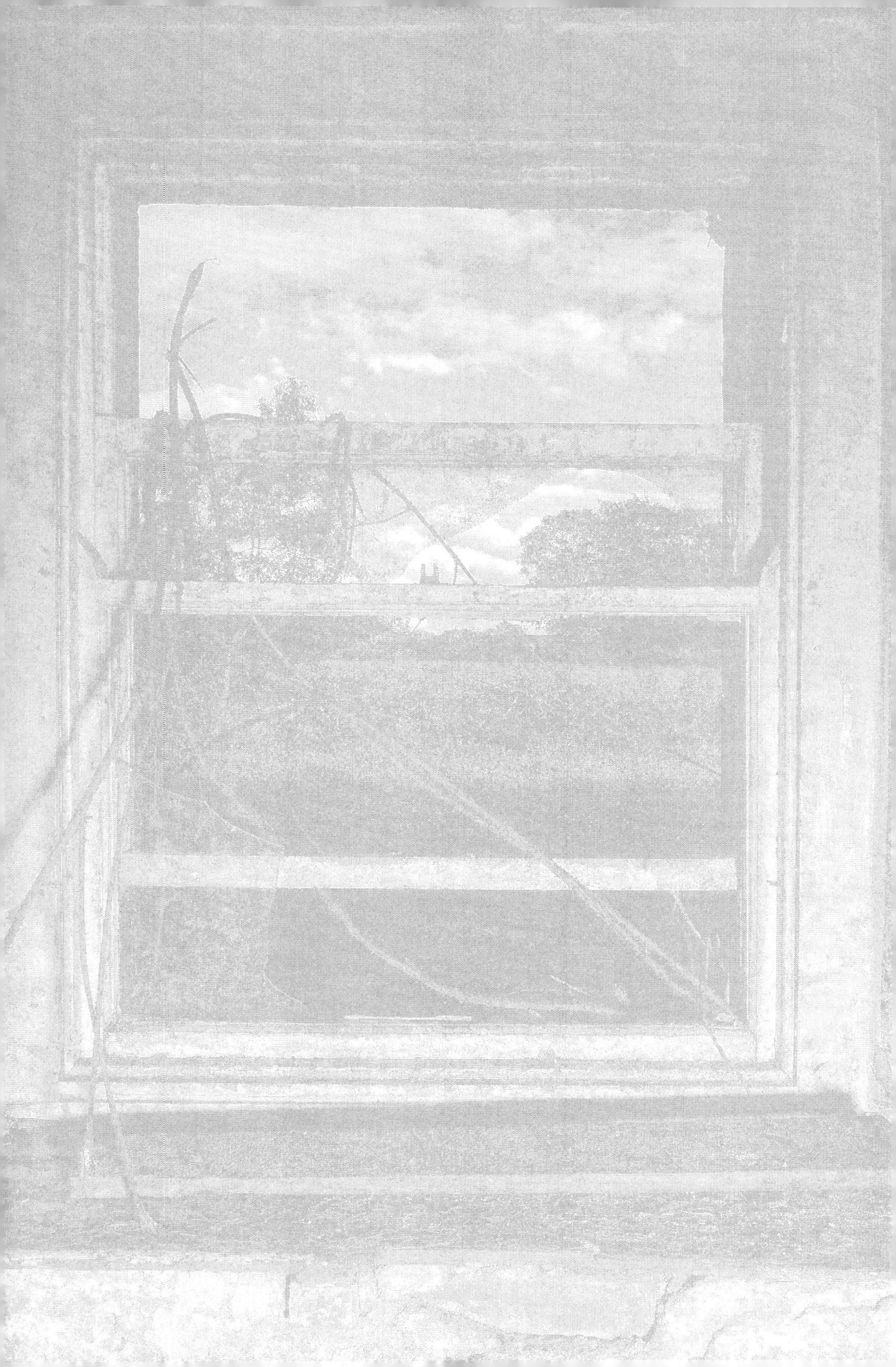

salmonpoetry

Cliffs of Moher, County Clare, Ireland

"Publishing the finest Irish and international literature."
Michael D. Higgins, President of Ireland